When Five Years Pass

By Federico García Lorca

Translated by Pilar Orti

When Five Years Pass

by Federico García Lorca

Translation by Pilar Orti

ISBN 978-1-4475-2715-2

Published by Unusual Connections Ltd, London, United
Kingdom

Translator's Introduction

I first saw 'When Five Years Pass' in Madrid in the late 1980's performed by the Spanish National Company, for 300 pesetas (yes, that's around £1.50) and I still remember it as one of the most exciting experiences in the theatre.

'When Five Years Pass' shows a side of Lorca that few people outside Spain (and inside?) know about. 'Blood Wedding', 'Yerma' and 'The House of Bernarda Alba' are well known throughout the world. They are also lyrical, but for most part, they are rooted in the real world. Their surrealist episodes seem more like interludes than part of the narrative. In 'When Five Years Pass', Lorca plays effortlessly with surrealism, a style he had to drop gradually in order to make his work more accessible to the wider public. If you want to see an even rougher side of the playwright, I suggest you read 'The Public' ('El Público') which I don't dare translate as its language is incredibly complex.

I have included in this introduction some notes on Federico García Lorca and 'When Five Years Pass' to put the work into contexct and also to offer my advice to those who want to perform or direct the play.

Thanks must go to Phillip and all at Forbidden for staging the piece, thanks to my mother who first introduced me to Lorca and to Bill Kosmas who has supported me throughout my Lorca-related ventures.

Federico García Lorca

"The most important thing about Federico was...
being Federico."
Jorge Guillén

Publishing his first book at the age of 20, the poet enjoyed great fame in his native Spain from an early age, as well as being loved by most people around him. In 1919 he moved away from his native Granada in the South of Spain, to Madrid to study law.

He lived at the Residencia de Madrid, a hall of residence where most of the intellectual figures of the time were staying. There he met and became friends with artists such as the painter Dalí, the future cinematographer Luis Buñuel, and the poet Alberti. Though Lorca had moved to Madrid to attend lectures which would lead him to completing his degree, he used to spend most of his time writing poetry and conversing in cafés. In Jose Luis Cano's words, he was "a burst of freedom and youth".

Jorge Guillén (Spanish poet and good friend of Lorca's) maintains that he was driven by a juvenile force. He managed to keep the child within, without adopting a childish attitude. Federico always got on well with children and seemed to have a special talent for understanding and communicating with them. It is therefore of no surprise that the song repertoire of every Spanish child contains at least one song written by him. Lorca seemed to be full of a desire to keep alive the spirit and essence of his childhood and was aware of it: *"The feelings from my childhood still lie within me. I don't seem to have left them."* (Cano)

And indeed, according to Margarita Ucelay's prologue to the play, 'When Five Years Pass' is full of childhood memories. She tells how Isabel García Lorca (his sister) can identify details from her younger years within the play: "the boys from the neighbourhood being capable of stoning any unfortunate animal that crossed their path, the sad tradition in our town of throwing dead cats to the river or to other people's roofs, his brothers dressed up as Harlequin and Clown during Carnival, ... the Mask costumes left for years in the family arks, and the chimes of the clock which Federico repeatedly used to alter, creating his own confusion with time and driving the maid crazy."

Having completed his degree, Lorca wrote to Jorge Guillén that he was beginning to feel guilty for not having followed the path his family would have liked him to and hence had decided to go for a professorship and maybe lecture on Spanish and Spain outside his country. This would not only keep his father happy, but would also allow him to leave the country, as he felt the need to get away.

Guillén managed to arrange for him to go to Paris to lecture. But this idea was soon abandoned and Federico found himself back in Spain, once more immersed in his writing.

In 1928, the first issue of the magazine "El Gallo" was published. It contained essays by Lorca and other writers including Guillén, and illustrations by artists such as Dalí. The magazine was certainly something new and had a touch of surrealism in it. In a letter to Sebastian Gash, Federico wrote, " *'El Gallo' in Granada has been a true scandal. Granada is a literary city and nothing new had ever happened in it. Therefore 'El Gallo' has produced a noise you'd never imagine"* (Cano). However, the magazine closed down after publishing its second issue. Later on in the year Lorca published his collection of poems which he had written four years earlier: 'El Romancero Gitano'. The book was a great success and bookshops were soon out of stock.

The happiness for which Lorca was known was due to his living life to the full with his five senses. But behind his constant smile there would be bursts of sadness and depression which only those close to him were aware of. In autumn 1928, in a letter to Jorge Guillén, he wrote: *"Fortunately, Autumn's coming. I have had a bad time myself. Very bad. One needs to have the amount of happiness God has given me not to succumb before the amount of conflicts that have lately jumped upon me.[...] You can't imagine what it is like spending a whole night at the balcony watching Granada at night, empty for me."*

It is no wonder therefore that in 1929, Lorca seized the opportunity presented to him by his teacher and friend Fernando de los Ríos to leave Spain.

New York

"I'll be in Madrid for two days... and I will immediately leave for Paris and London, from where I will travel to New York. Are you surprised? I'm killing myself with laughter with this decision. But it will suit me and it is important for my life... New York seems horrible to me and that is why I'm going there. I think I'll have a good time."
Letter to his friend Carlos Morla (1929)

Lorca felt welcome wherever he went during his stay in New York. Although he enrolled in English lessons as soon as he arrived, he never attended them and left the country with as little knowledge of the language as when he first set foot in the country.

He was a popular figure amongst the Hispanic community in New York. His name was already well known and he had several friends in the city to take care of him.

After two and a half months in New York, Federico had spent most of his time going for walks, going to the cinema, theatre and jazz cafés and talking to his friends. He would stay up all night writing in his room of the halls of residence and then would sleep during most of the day, being referred to as the "sleepy boy" by the cleaners at the hall.

Just before the start of the Autumn term, Lorca visited Angel del Río, a poet friend of his who was teaching at Columbia University. According to del Río, Lorca spent most of his time writing, and it was during this period that he commenced 'When Five Years Pass'.

When Five Years Pass: the Play

"One must not wait. One must live."

As if thinking that he will be able to make time stand still, the Young Man delays his marriage for five years. He is so in love with the image he had of his Bride, that he does not doubt for a moment that five years might be a long period for her to wait, during which she might change her mind.

In the opening act we meet the Old Man, friend of the protagonist. Not wanting to give in to the convention of time, he makes up his own expressions - thus his *twenty snowfalls*, and *remembering towards tomorrow*. It seems like the Old Man has been trying to prevent the Young Man from taking action - as soon as the Young Man decides to look for the Typist, the Old Man is wounded as he has not been able make the Young Man wait any longer.

Friends 1 and 2 on the other hand have a different view of life. Friend 1 lives life to the full, keeping himself busy all the time. This prevents him from thinking too much and taking life too seriously. Friend 2 avoids facing reality and the problems and responsibilities of growing up by wanting time to remain still and trying to stay a child.

In one of the most beautifully sad scenes ever written, the fear of death is portrayed in the simplicity innate to both its characters: the dead Boy and the dead Cat. The latter has been stoned to death by a pack of boys and yet her innocence remains: she is still willing to talk to a boy and even look for his care. The little boy has not suffered much: his mother weeps for his death (there is never a mention of the father) and many people attend his funeral. But whatever their situation was on Earth, both are now experiencing fear of the unknown.

The theme of death flows through 'When Five Years Pass' as through most of Lorca's works. It was something that thoroughly intrigued him. Martinez Nadal remembers once being asked by the poet: "After the transition, what do you think will happen? Will the dead feel they are dead or will there be a life of the dead?" (*Nadal*). References to the Dead Boy and Cat are made throughout the play, continuously reminding us of the inevitability of death.

Five years pass between the first two acts and we learn that the Bride, far from waiting around like her fiancée, has decided to take a lover who will treat her (or who will allow her to feel) like the woman she is now and not the innocent girl she was five years ago. She is not interested in ideas and intellectualising - that is why she prefers the American Football Player's grip to the Young Man's books. While the Maid, full of romanticism, tries to convince her that what she is doing is wrong, the Bride feels she must run away from her current life if she is to live at all.

Her Father, old fashioned, does not understand his daughter's new attitude. He is immersed in his own astronomical world - like many people he is more interested in those things out of reach that in those "under our brows".

Eventually, the inevitable happens and the Young Man has to confront that he has wasted five years while his bride was learning to live. About to carry on making the same mistake of doing nothing to change his luck, the Mannequin of the Bride's wedding dress appears and reminds him that if he is to carry on living (not only as a man but also as the vehicle for his genes to pass on to the next generation) he is to look for his old Typist who was in love with him. She had not wasted her time and had repeatedly told him how much she loved him in the hope that he would seize the opportunity of loving someone who was actually present instead of loving someone in his mind.

Act III is introduced by the Harlequin and the Clown who present the final events as if they were part of a circus act: they introduce the Mask, who was actually the mother of the Dead boy in the first act. She explains how she left her lover, but later on we realise that she has been twisting the facts around to how she would have liked things to have been. Like the Mask, the Typist has changed all her memories to fit her wishes as to how her relationship with her loved one should have been.

The Young Man finds his former typist. This time, unlike the Young Man, she does get her dream but, like the Girl at the beginning of the act, she is too scared of reality and decides to evade it by postponing going with the Young Man for another five years.

Battered and exhausted the Young Man returns home. After his long journey, his own house seems small. The dialogue is slow, he does not seem to be able to remember some facts, he is irritable with Juan.... even the colours in this scene are dull. As opposed to the first act when he was visited by his friends in vivid colours, this time his visitors are dressed in black and white. (There is an urban myth that says that if you stop dreaming in colour you die, and indeed, this is just what happens in this scene: the dream becomes a nightmare.)

At the end of the play, the clock strikes twelve, (or is it still striking six, only this time we hear its echo?) and everything seems to return to normal as if it had all happenned in the Young Man's mind, or as if time had never passed.

When Five Years Pass: What the critics said

'The Public' was finished in 1930 and 'When Five Years Pass' in 1931. None of the first readings of either of these plays were greeted with enthusiasm.

The author Carlos Morla, who hosted the first reading of 'When Five Years Pass' admitted in his diary that he had not understood the play. Neither did the actress Margarita Xirgu, who enjoyed a great friendship with the author, when the poet himself read her the play. She could not quite picture it and thought it would be impossible to produce in the theatre. It was therefore not until 1933 that he even dared offer the script to a theatre group for performance.

After Lorca's death, most critics showed themselves quite negative towards the play. They thought that before having enjoyed great success with his tragedies, he had gone down the wrong path when writing this play and that it was impossible to transfer to the stage: all in all it was just a poor attempt at surrealism. Other critics labelled it as just a rough draft, not even worth judging. On the other hand, later critics suggest that a careful study of the play and its production on the stage are necessary before forming an opinion.

And indeed, the play was successfully produced by many alternative and university theatre groups in Puerto Rico (1954), Paris (1959) and the English version in New York in 1960. But it wasn't until 1988 that the play was finally produced by the Spanish National Company in Madrid, where it played to full houses.

With the publication of 'The Public' in 1976, the critics were able to observe the connection between the two plays, which allowed them to finally see the author's objectives in using this little accepted style.

Federico García Lorca on theatre

"Theatre is one of the most expressive and useful instruments for the edification of a country and a barometer which measures its grandness or decline. A sensitive theatre and well orientated in all its branches can change in only a few years the sensitivity of a nation."

The different styles of theatre he encountered in New York had a vast influence on Lorca. He was described as a sort of sponge, able to absorb and make his the different styles and tendencies around him. It is not surprising therefore that his most innovative work was produced during his stay in New York. *"The new theatre, advanced in both form and theory is my greatest concern. New York is a unique place to feel the pulse of the new theatrical art".* (Morales)

But Lorca himself was aware of the little acceptability that this new style of theatre would be greeted with. The first reading of 'When Five Years Pass' was greeted with apparently less enthusiasm than other works and even later on, many critics still labelled it as "incomplete" or saw it as a step back in his work. Aware of this scepticism, Lorca decided to change his path to a more popular style thus preparing the ground for what he thought would be his greatest works.

"In these 'impossible comedies' lies my true objective. But to show true character and deserve everyone's respect, I have given other things." (Morales)

This was a style he could only give up gradually, and in the final act of 'Blood Wedding', we find a scene between the Moon and Death, as symbols of fatality. The realism of previous acts disappears here, allowing poetry and symbolism to take over. This was the poet's favourite part of this tragedy, the most theatrical moment: that in which poetic fantasy took first place, a style with which he felt like "fish in the water". And how right he had been in predicting the criticism of his most favourite style: the one reservation the critics seemed to have about 'Blood Wedding' was the personification of the Moon *(Edwards)*.

A Southern Spaniard, brought up in a middle class family, one of his main objectives was to bring theatre, especially the classics, to the people. To this purpose he set up the University Dramatic Group *La Barraca* in 1932 which would tour the Spanish towns. The project soon found much support from the University and the government. Students and non professionals would tour the country in this Barraca (Spanish for 'cart').

Lorca believed in presenting classical works in a simple way which would allow the audience to find their relevance to modern times. The first plays to be presented were two 'entremeses' from the great Spanish writer Miguel de Cervantes (best known for his 'Don Quixote'). Other works produced included Calderón's "Life's a Dream" and Lope de Vega's "Fuenteovejuna". He believed that theatre could not be labelled as "old" or "new" but only as good or bad.

"Theatre will continue to be theatre while it walks in step with its time, gathering the emotions, the pains, the fights and the dramas of that era. Theatre must portray the drama of current life."

Though he did not abandon his writing while setting up and running *La Barraca,* he did feel as attached to it and invested as much time in it as in his other works. *"La Barraca is the whole of my work for me, the work that interests me, which excites me, more than my literary work; many are the times when I have stopped writing a line or finishing a piece for its sake."* (Cano)

Lorca, the "dramatic poet" who was a poet before he became a playwright, always believed that it was the dramatic work of poets which survived through the ages - works not necessarily in verse, but poetic in essence.

In one of his later interviews, with González Deleito, he showed his sadness at the loss of romanticism, which had been replaced on the stage world wide by the new forms: naturalism and realism. *"Naturalism and modernism have cleared up all romantic germs."* He believed these new styles had transformed both audiences and practitioners making them less sensitive to the strong passions carried by poetry. *"People say about recited verse today: "It rhymes so well, it sounds so good!" But no one cries, no one feels the tears in their eyes."*

And when asked which was the favourite of his dramatic works, he replied:

"I can't say I prefer any of my all ready performed pieces. I am in love with those I haven't written yet."

Although he never involved himself directly in politics, it was a well known fact that Federico García Lorca's views were close to those of the Republican party. When in July 1936, the Civil War broke out in Spain, Lorca left Madrid to return to Granada, even though his friends insisted that he would be saffer in the capital. On the 16 August he was taken away by Franco's men, after promising they were only going to question him. On the morning of the 19 August 1936, exactly five years after he completed 'When Five Years Pass', Federico García Lorca was shot, becoming just another victim of the Spanish Civil War.

Performing Lorca

Performing Lorca is never easy for the actor - he used to create his own world through his language, a mixture of poetry in both verse and prose. The challenge for the modern actor is to stylise his/her performance in a way that matches the language, while still being true to the character and emotions that the words portray.

A practical note: I have left the Spanish word 'Ay' untranslated. This word is an exclamation: it has stronger connotations than 'Oh!' and sometimes is used as 'Ouch' or as an expression of severe pain. It does not mean 'yes' as in the old English word. If it feels strange to pronounce, it can be changed to 'Oh' or a sigh of despair or pain. The word is used repeatedly in the Maid/Bride scene and there, its pronunciation needs to stay consistent to keep the rhythm of the dialogue.

In all my translations of Lorca's work, I have always tried to keep the rhythm and poetic nature of his work. Reading the English text should feel slightly alien, just as alien as reading the Spanish text will be to the Spanish speaker. 'When Five Years Pass' is an explosion of surrealism - in the characters created, the timeframe and of course, the language.

With a scene between a dead boy and dead cat, a mannequin that speaks and a silent American football player who chain-smokes cigars, 'When Five Years Pass' is deliciously difficult to perform - that is, until you surrender to its language and its style.

Pilar Orti

Bibliography

Jose Luis Cano *García Lorca* (1988)
Gwynne Edwards *Lorca: the theatre beneath the sand* (1995)
Nicolás González Deleito *Federico García Lorca y el teatro de hoy* (1935) Obras completas AGUILAR (1954)
Jorge Guillén *Federico en persona*   Obras completas AGUILAR (1954)
Rafael Martinez Nadal. *"El público" Amor y muerte en la obra de Federico García Lorca* (1988)
Felipe Morales *Al habla con Federico García Lorca* (April 1936) Obras completas AGUILAR (1954)
Margarita Ucelay. Prologue to *Así que Pasen Cinco Años* CATEDRA (1995)

When Five Years Pass

By Federico García Lorca

When Five Years Pass

List of characters

Young man

Old man

A dead boy

A dead cat

Juan, a valet

Friend 1

Friend 2

The Typist

The Bride

The Mannequin wearing the Bride's dress

The American Football Player

The Maid

The Bride's Father

Clown

Harlequin

Girl

The Mask

Player 1

Player 2

Player 3

Other masked characters

When Five Years Pass

ACT I

A library. The YOUNG MAN is sitting down. He's wearing blue pyjamas. The OLD MAN wears a grey suit, with a white beard and big golden spectacles, also sitting down.

YOUNG MAN

     I'm not surprised.

OLD MAN

     Excuse me...

YOUNG MAN

     The same thing happens to me.

OLD MAN *(inquisitive and kind)*

     Really?

YOUNG MAN

     Yes.

OLD MAN

     Well, it's...

YOUNG MAN

     I remember...

OLD MAN *(laughing)*

     One's always remembering...

YOUNG MAN

     I...

OLD MAN *(eager)*

     Go on...

YOUNG MAN

I'd keep the sweets from dinner so I could eat them later.

OLD MAN

Later? They taste better. So did I.

YOUNG MAN

And I remember one day...

OLD MAN *(interrupting passionately)*

I love the word remember. It's a green word, it's juicy. It seems to sprout threads of cool water.

YOUNG MAN *(gaily, trying to convince himself)*

Yes, yes, of course. You're right. One must fight all notion of decay, like the plaster falling off the wall. Many times I've got up in the middle of the night to tear out the garden grass. I don't want grass growing in my house, or broken furniture.

OLD MAN

Right. Or broken furniture because one must remember, but...

YOUNG MAN

But one must remember things which are alive, intact, boiling in their blood.

OLD MAN

Well done! I mean *(lowering his voice)* one must remember. But remember in advance.

YOUNG MAN

In advance?

OLD MAN *(carefully)*

One must remember towards tomorrow.

YOUNG MAN *(engrossed)*

Towards tomorrow!

(A clock strikes six. The TYPIST crosses the stage, crying in silence)

OLD MAN

    Six o'clock.

YOUNG MAN

    Yes, six o'clock and it's too hot. *(He rises)* There's a stormy sky. Beautiful. Covered in grey clouds...

OLD MAN

    So it turns out you...? I was a great friend of that family. The father's in particular.. He's into astronomy. *(Ironically)* Not bad, eh? Astronomy. What about her?

YOUNG MAN

    I don't know much about her. But it doesn't matter. I think she loves me.

OLD MAN

    Sure!

YOUNG MAN

    They left on a long trip. I was almost happy...

OLD MAN

    Did her father ever come here?

YOUNG MAN

    Never! He can't, not yet... For reasons which needn't be explained. I won't marry her...till five years pass.

OLD MAN

    Well done! *(Happily)*

YOUNG MAN *(seriously)*

    Why do you say well done?

OLD MAN

Well, because... Is this beautiful? *(pointing at the room)*

YOUNG MAN

No.

OLD MAN

Doesn't the time of departure, the events, what must happen now, cause you great distress?

YOUNG MAN

Yes, yes. Don't talk about it.

OLD MAN

What's going on in the streets?

YOUNG MAN

Noise, always noise, dust, heat, bad smells. I don't like things from the street coming into my home. *(A long moan is heard. Pause.)* Juan, close that window.

(A subtle servant who tiptoes closes the window)

OLD MAN

She... is young.

YOUNG MAN

Very young. Fifteen years old!

OLD MAN

I don't like that way of expressing oneself. Fifteen years she's lived though, which are herself. But why can't we say fifteen snowfalls, fifteen winds, fifteen twilights? Won't you dare run away? Fly? Expand your love all over the sky?

YOUNG MAN *(sitting down and covering his face with his hands)*

I love her too much!

OLD MAN *(standing up and energetically)*

> Or why not say fifteen roses, fifteen wings, or fifteen grains of sand. Won't you dare concentrate, make striking yet small, that love living in your chest?

YOUNG MAN

> You want to pull me away from her. But I know your ways. One need only observe a live insect on one's hand, or watch the sea carefully noting the shape of each wave, for the face or wound we carry in our hearts to turn to foam. But I'm in love with her, as she is with me, and that's why I can wait five years to wrap myself at night, when all the world's in darkness, with her bright plaits around my neck.

OLD MAN

> May I remind you that your girlfriend... has no plaits.

YOUNG MAN *(irritated)*

> I know. She cut them off without my consent and this *(in agony)* changes my perception of her. *(Energetically)* I know she has no plaits. *(Almost furious)* Why did you remind me? *(sadly)* But she'll grow them back in these next five years.

OLD MAN *(enthusiastically)*

> And more beautiful than ever. They'll be a pair of plaits...

YOUNG MAN

> They are, they are. *(Happily)*

OLD MAN

> They are a pair of plaits whose perfume is enough to keep you alive without bread or water.

YOUNG MAN *(getting up)*

> I think about her so much!

OLD MAN

> Dream so much!

YOUNG MAN

> What?

OLD MAN

> You dream so much that...

YOUNG MAN

> My flesh is bare. Everything inside me is one wound.

OLD MAN

> Drink.

YOUNG MAN

> Thank you! If I start thinking about the young girl, about my girl.

OLD MAN

> Say my bride. I dare you!

YOUNG MAN

> Bride... you know, if I say 'bride' I immediately see her suspended from the sky by enormous plaits made of snow. No, she's not my bride, *(He makes a move as if trying to push away the image that wants to take over)* She's my girl, my young girl.

OLD MAN

> Go on, go on.

YOUNG MAN

> Well if I start thinking about her, I draw her. I make her move, fair and alive, but suddenly, who changes her nose, or breaks her teeth, or turns her into one dressed in rags, wandering like a monster round my thoughts, as if she were looking at her reflection in a broken mirror?

OLD MAN

Who? It's surprising you should ask who. Things under our eyes change more than those under our brow. The water flowing into the river is completely different to that leaving it. And, who remembers the exact map of a sandy desert... or the face of an old friend?

YOUNG MAN

Yes, yes. What lies inside us is more alive, even if it's changing. You see, the last time I saw her I couldn't look closely at her because she had two little wrinkles on her forehead, which, subconsciously, would... do you understand? They would fill her face and make her crumpled, old, as if she'd suffered much. I had to pull away to... focus! that's the word, within my heart.

OLD MAN

When you saw her looking old, was she totally devoted to you?

YOUNG MAN

Yes.

OLD MAN

Totally dominated by you?

YOUNG MAN

Yes.

OLD MAN

And if in that instant, she had confessed that she'd cheated on you, that she didn't love you, her wrinkles would have turned into the most delicate rose in the world.

YOUNG MAN

Yes.

OLD MAN

And you would you have loved her more for that?

YOUNG MAN

Yes, yes.

OLD MAN

Then? *(He laughs)*

YOUNG MAN

Then... living is very hard.

OLD MAN

That's why one must fly from one thing to another until one is lost. If she is fifteen years old, she can also be fifteen dusks, and higher we go! Things are more alive if they're within us, than if they're out there, exposed to the air or death. That's why we... don't... go... or we wait. Because to do otherwise is to die now, and it's more beautiful to think that tomorrow we'll still see those hundred golden horns with which the sun lifts the clouds.

YOUNG MAN

(Shaking his hand) Thank you, thank you, for everything!

OLD MAN

I'll come back.

(The TYPIST appears)

YOUNG MAN

Did you finish those letters?

TYPIST

(Crying) Yes, sir.

OLD MAN

(To the YOUNG MAN) What's up with her?

TYPIST

I'd like to leave this house.

OLD MAN

> That's easy, isn't it?

YOUNG MAN

> *(Dazed)* You know best...

TYPIST

> I want to, but I can't.

YOUNG MAN

> *(Sweetly)* I'm not keeping you. You know there's nothing I can do. I've asked you sometimes to wait, but you...

TYPIST

> But I won't wait, what does waiting mean?

OLD MAN

> *(Serious)* And why not? Waiting is believing and living.

TYPIST

> I won't wait because I don't feel I can and because I don't want to and yet I can't get away from here.

YOUNG MAN

> You always end up giving no reason!

TYPIST

> What reasons have I to give? There is just one reason and that's... I love you! Always have. Don't be scared, sir. When you were a child I used to watch you from my balcony. One day you fell, and bled at the knee, remember? That live blood still trembles like a red serpent within my breasts.

OLD MAN

> That's not right. Blood is dry, and the past is the past.

TYPIST

> I'm not to blame, sir! *(To the YOUNG MAN)* Please give me my money. I want to leave this house.

YOUNG MAN

>*(Irritated)* All right. I won't be blamed either. And you know perfectly well I'm not my own master. You may go.

TYPIST

>Did you hear that? He's throwing me out of his house. He doesn't want me here.

(She leaves, crying)

OLD MAN *(Cautiously, to the YOUNG MAN)*

>That woman is dangerous.

YOUNG MAN

>I'd love to love her the same way I'd love to be thirsty in front of a fountain. I'd love to...

OLD MAN

>No way. What would you do tomorrow? Eh? Think. Tomorrow.

FRIEND 1

>*(Entering noisily)* Such silence in this house! What for? Give me some water. With ice and anisette! *(The OLD MAN leaves)* A cocktail.

YOUNG MAN

>I suppose you'd like to break the furniture.

FRIEND 1

>A lonely man, a serious man, in this heat!

YOUNG MAN

>Won't you sit down?

FRIEND 1

>*(Taking him in his arms, and spinning him around)* Ring a ring a roses *etc.*

YOUNG MAN

Leave me alone! I'm not in the mood.

FRIEND 1

Ooooh! Who was that old man? A friend of yours? And where do you keep the pictures of the women you sleep with? Look, *(drawing near)* I'm going to grab you by the collar and put some blush on those cheeks of wax, or rub them as so.

YOUNG MAN

(Irritated) Leave me alone!

FRIEND 1

And then I'll throw you out into the street.

YOUNG MAN

And what will I do there? What ever you want? I have enough with listening to its cars and confused people.

FRIEND 1

(Sitting down on the sofa and stretching out) Aaah! Mmmm! I however... I made three conquests yesterday and as the day before I made two, and one today, then... I can't keep any of them, because I have no time. I was with a girl... Ernestina, would you like to meet her?

YOUNG MAN

No.

FRIEND 1

(Getting up) Nooo and full stop. If you could see... she has a waist... no... Matilde has a better waist. *(On impulse)*. Look, it's a waist fit for all arms and so fragile one wishes for an axe in one's hand to slice it up.

YOUNG MAN

(Distracted, not following the conversation) I'll go upstairs then.

FRIEND 1

>*(Laying on his front)* I have no time, I have no time, everything's piling up. Because, look, I date Ernestina, *(getting up)* her plaits are so, tight, very dark and then...

YOUNG MAN

>*(He bangs his fist on the table)* You're not letting me think!

FRIEND 1

>But you don't need to think! I'm leaving. No matter... how... *(looking at his watch)* Time's gone. Terrible, always the same thing. I have no time and I'm sorry. I was with an ugly woman. Do you hear me? Ha, ha, ha. Very ugly, but adorable. One of those brunettes one misses at noon on a summer day. And I like her *(throwing a cushion in the air)* because she's like a lion tamer.

YOUNG MAN

>Enough!

FRIEND 1

>Don't get angry, but a woman can be ugly and a lion tamer beautiful, and the other way round and.. what do we know? *(He fills a cocktail glass)*

YOUNG MAN

>Nothing.

FRIEND 1

>Won't you tell me what's up with you?

YOUNG MAN

>Nothing. Don't you know me? This is how I am.

FRIEND 1

>I don't understand, I don't understand but I can't be serious. *(He laughs)* I'll salute you like the Chinese. *(He rubs his nose against the other's)*

YOUNG MAN

(Smiling) Get off!

FRIEND 1

Laugh! (He tickles him)

YOUNG MAN

(Laughing) Barbarian! (They fight)

FRIEND 1

Missed!

YOUNG MAN

I can win.

FRIEND 1

Gotcha. (He grabs him with his head between his legs and hits him on the head)

OLD MAN

(Entering gravely) Excuse me... (The young men are standing) Excuse me... (Energetically, looking at the YOUNG MAN) I'll forget my hat.

FRIEND 1

(Amazed) What?

OLD MAN

(Furious) Yes, sir! I'll forget my hat... (mumbling) I mean, I forgot my hat.

FRIEND 1

Aaaaah! (Crashing of glass is heard)

YOUNG MAN

(Loudly) Juan! Close the windows.

FRIEND 1

A bit of a storm. I hope it's loud.

YOUNG MAN

I don't want to know! (Loudly) Everything well closed.

FRIEND 1

You'll have to hear the thunder.

YOUNG MAN

Or not!

FRIEND 1

You will.

YOUNG MAN

I don't care what goes on outside but this is my house and no one's allowed in.

OLD MAN

(Outraged at the friend) That's an irrefutable truth.

(Distant thunder)

FRIEND 1

(Passionately) Everyone who wants to will come in, maybe not right here, but under your bed. *(Closer thunder)*

YOUNG MAN

(Shouting) But not now! Not now!

OLD MAN

Bravo!

FRIEND 1

Open the window! I'm hot.

OLD MAN

It will be opened.

YOUNG MAN

Later!

FRIEND 1

But hang on... could you tell me...?

(Another thunder is heard. Light dims and a blue stormy light invades the scene. The three characters hide behind the screen.

The DEAD BOY appears with the CAT. The BOY is dressed in white, with a crown of white roses on his head. The CAT is blue with two blood stains on its chest. The BOY is holding one of the CAT's paws.)

CAT

Meow.

BOY

Chsst.

CAT

Meeeooow.

BOY

Take my white hankie.

Take my white crown.

Cry no more.

CAT

My wounds hurt,

Those the boys made on my back.

BOY

My heart hurts too.

CAT

Boy, why does it hurt? Say.

BOY

Because it's not ticking.

It stopped yesterday, very slowly, nightingale of my bed.
So much fuss. You should have seen! They placed me
With these roses under the window.

CAT

And what did you feel?

BOY

I felt fountains and bees round the room.
They tied my hands together. Wrongly done!
The boys looked at me through the glass
And a man with a hammer on my shell nailed paper stars.
(Crossing his hands) No angels came. No. Cat.

CAT

Don't call me "cat".

BOY

No?

CAT

I'm a lady cat.

BOY

You're a lady cat?

CAT

(Coy) You should've known.

BOY

Why?

CAT

By my silver voice.

BOY

(Gallantly) Won't you sit down?

CAT

Yes. I'm hungry.

BOY

I'll try to catch a rat. *(He looks under the chairs. The cat, sitting on a stool, shivers)* Don't eat it all.

Only a paw,

because you're very weak.

CAT

Ten stones the boys threw at me.

BOY

They're as heavy as the roses

Which last night oppressed my throat.

Would you like one? *(He takes a rose from his head)*

CAT

(Gaily) I'd like one.

BOY

With your stains of wax, white rose,

You look like the eye of the broken moon,

Faint gazelle amongst the broken glass.

(He puts in on)

CAT

What were you doing?

BOY

Playing. And you?

CAT

Playing!

Along the roof I walked about,

Snub nosed cat, with tinny snout.

In the morning

I'd grab the fish in the stream,

And at noon

Under the rosebush I'd sleep.

BOY

And at night?

CAT

(Emphatic) I'd go on my own.

BOY

With no one?

CAT

Down the forest.

BOY

(Happy) So did I. Ay, snub nosed cat,

with tinny snout!

To eat the blackberries and apples.

And I'd go with the children

to play our game.

CAT

What game?

BOY

Licking the nails on the door.

CAT

And was it nice?

BOY

No, lady cat,

like sucking pennies. *(Distant thunder)*

Ay! Wait! Aren't they coming? I'm scared.

You know? I ran away from home. (Sniffing)

I don't want them to bury me.

Lace and glass decorate my box.

It'd be better if I slept

Among the reeds in the water.

I don't want them to bury me. Let's go now!

(He pulls her by the paw)

CAT

They're going to bury us? When?

BOY

Tomorrow.

In some dark holes.

They all weep. They're all quiet.

But they leave. I saw it.

And then, you know...?

CAT

What happens then?

BOY

They'll eat us up.

CAT

Who?

BOY

The crocodile and his wife

With their children, who are many.

CAT

And what do they eat?

BOY

>The face,

>The fingers and *(lowering his voice)* and the willy.

CAT

>*(Offended)* I don't have a willy.

BOY *(Energetic)*

>Lady cat!

>They'll eat your little paws and whiskers.

>*(Very distant thunder)*

>Let's go. From house to house,

>We'll get to where the sea horses graze.

>It's not the Heavens. It's hard earth,

>With many crickets that sing,

>With grass dancing in the wind,

>With slings that stones can swing

>And wind that like a sword stings.

>I want to be a boy! A boy!

(He starts to exit)

CAT

>The door is closed.

>Let's go down the staircase.

BOY

>They'll see us down the staircase.

CAT

>Wait.

BOY

They're coming to bury us!

CAT

Let's go through the window.

BOY

We'll never again see the light,

Nor the clouds slowly forming,

Nor the crickets in the grass,

Or the wind become a sword.

(Crossing his hands)

Ay, sunflower!

Ay, sunflower of fire!

Ay, sunflower!

CAT

Ay, pink carnation of the sun!

BOY

Burning he travels through the sky,

Through the hills of coal and sea,

Like a dove stilled by the sand,

With broken winds and a flower in its beak.

(Singing) And on that flower an olive,

And on that olive a lemon...

How does it go...? I can't remember, how does it go?

CAT

Ay, sunflower

Sunflower of the morning small

BOY

Ay, pink carnation of the sun!

(There is barely any light. The BOY and CAT walk separately, feeling their way)

CAT

    There's no light. Where are you?

BOY

    Shush!

CAT

    Boy, will the crocodiles come?

BOY

    No.

CAT

    Did you find the exit?

(The CAT is near one of the doors when a hand appears and drags her offstage. She screams from within)

CAT

    Boy! Boy! *(In agony)* Boy! Boy!

(The BOY walks terrified, stopping at every step)

BOY

    (Softly) She drowned.

    A hand took her away.

    It must belong to God.

    Don't bury me! Wait a few minutes...

    As I pull the petals off!

    (He takes a flower from his head)

I'll go on my own, very slowly,

And then you'll let me look at the sun...

Just a little, a ray will do.

(Pulling the petals off) Yes, no, yes, no, yes.

VOICE

No. NO.

BOY

I always said no!

(A hand appears and pulls the BOY, who faints. As he disappears, the light returns to its original state. The three characters appear from behind the scene. They are hot and shaken. The YOUNG MAN has a blue fan, the OLD one, black, and the FRIEND an aggressive red one. They fan themselves.)

OLD MAN

There's more to come.

YOUNG MAN

Yes, later.

FRIEND 1

That's enough. I don't think you can escape the storm.

VOICE *offstage*

My son! My son!

YOUNG MAN

God it's late! Juan, who's screams like that?

JUAN

(Always entering smoothly and on tiptoe) The housekeeper's son died and they're going to bury him. His mother cries.

FRIEND 1

Naturally!

OLD MAN

Yes, but the past is past.

FRIEND 1

But it's happening.

(They argue)

JUAN

Sir, would you be kind enough to lend me your bedroom key?

YOUNG MAN

What for?

JUAN

The boys killed a cat and threw it on the garden roof. It needs to be removed.

YOUNG MAN

(Annoyed) Here. *(To the old man)* You won't beat him.

OLD MAN

I'm not interested.

FRIEND 1

That's not true. He's interested. It's me who's not interested, because I know for sure that snow is cold and fire burns.

OLD MAN

(Ironically) It depends.

FRIEND 1

(To the YOUNG MAN) He's fooling you.

(The OLD MAN looks energetically at the FRIEND, squashing his hat.)

YOUNG MAN

> *(Strong)* He has no effect on me. This is how I am. But you can't understand that I can wait five years for a woman, bursting with a love that burns and grows every day.

FRIEND 1

> There's no need to wait!

YOUNG MAN

> Do you think I can win over material things, over obstacles that arise and increase, without causing others any pain?

FRIEND 1

> You come before anyone else!

YOUNG MAN

> By waiting, the knot unties and the fruit ripens.

FRIEND 1

> I'd rather eat it green, or better still, I'd rather cut off one of its flowers and place it in my lapel.

OLD MAN

> That's not true!

FRIEND 1

> You are too old to know!

OLD MAN

> *(Smoothly)* I fought all my life to shine a light in the darkest place. And while people wrung a dove's neck, I held its hand and helped it fly.

FRIEND 1

And naturally the hunter starved to death!

(FRIEND 2 enters through a door in the left. He's dressed in white in an impeccable woollen suit with gloves and shoes of the same colour. If this character cannot be played by a very young man, it will be played by a woman. Of exaggerated style, the buttons on the suit are big and blue and the waistcoat and tie will be of ruffled lace)

FRIEND 2

Bless the times when there is toasted bread, oil and sleep. A lot of sleep. Let it never end. I heard you.

YOUNG MAN

(Amazed) How did you get in?

FRIEND 2

Somehow. Through the window. Two children, friends of mine, helped me. I've known them since I was a child and they pushed me by the feet. There's going to be a downpour... but a nice one fell last year. There was so little light my hands turned yellow. *(To the OLD MAN)* Do you remember?

OLD MAN

(Bitter) I don't remember anything.

FRIEND 2

(To FRIEND 1) And you?

FRIEND 1

(Serious) Neither do I!

FRIEND 2

I was very young, but I remember every detail.

FRIEND 1

    Look...

FRIEND 2

    That's why I don't want to see this one. Rain is beautiful. At school it used to come in through the courtyard and it would crash against the walls those very small naked women it carries inside. Have you never seen them? When I was five... no, when I was two... I lie! One, just one. It's beautiful, isn't it? Right? One year! I took one of those small women of the rain and kept her in a fishbowl for two days.

FRIEND 1

    (With irony) And she grew?

FRIEND 2

    No! She turned smaller, younger, as it should be, as is fair, until there was nothing left except one raindrop. And she'd sing a song...

I'm back for my wings,

Allow me to return.

I want to die being dawn break,

I want to die being yesterday.

I'm back for my wings,

Allow me to return

I want to die being a spring,

I want to die outside the sea...

Which is exactly what I sing all the time.

OLD MAN

    (Irritated, to the YOUNG MAN) He's completely crazy.

FRIEND 2

    (Hearing this) Crazy, because I don't want to be full of pain and wrinkles like you. Because I want to live what's

mine but they're taking it away. I don't know you. I don't want to see people like you.

FRIEND 1

(Drinking) All that is nothing but fear of death.

FRIEND 2

No. Just now, before coming here, I saw a boy they were going to bury under the first drops of rain. That's how I want to be buried. In a box that small but you want to argue in this downpour. But this face is mine and you are taking it away from me. I was tender and used to sing, and now there is a man, a gentleman *(to the OLD MAN)* like you, walking inside me with two or three masks ready for me. *(He brings out a mirror and looks at himself)* But not yet; I can still see myself up the cherry trees... with that grey suit... a grey suit with silver hooks... My God! *(He covers his face with his hands)*

OLD MAN

Suits get torn, hooks get rusty, but we carry on.

FRIEND 2

Oh please don't talk like that!

OLD MAN

(Enthusiastic) Houses sink.

FRIEND 1

(Energetic and defensively) Houses don't sink.

OLD MAN

(Unshaken) Eyes are put out, and a very sharp sickle cuts the reeds on the shore.

FRIEND 2

(Calm) Of course! All that happens later on.

OLD MAN

On the contrary. All that's happened all ready.

FRIEND 2

> Everything behind remains still. How come you don't know? One must softly wake everything up. If not, in four or five years time, there will be a well into which we'll all fall.

OLD MAN

> *(Furious)* Silence!

YOUNG MAN

> *(Trembling, to the OLD MAN)* Did you hear that?

OLD MAN

> Too clearly. *(He quickly leaves)*

YOUNG MAN

> *(Going after him)* Where are you going? Why do you leave like that? Wait! *(He leaves after him)*

FRIEND 2

> *(Shrugging)* All right. He's old. You, however, have not complained.

FRIEND 1

> *(Who's been drinking non stop)* No.

FRIEND 2

> You have enough with your drink.

FRIEND 1

> *(Serious, with a drunken face)* I do what I please. What I think is right. I didn't ask for your opinion.

FRIEND 2

> *(Scared)* Yes, yes... And I'm not saying a word. *(He sits on the sofa)*

(FRIEND 1 downs two drinks, to the very end, and hitting his forehead as if remembering something, suddenly exits. JUAN enters, always delicate on tiptoe. It begins to rain.)

FRIEND 2

>The downpour. *(He looks at his hands)* What an ugly light. *(He falls asleep)*

YOUNG MAN

>*(Entering)* He'll be back tomorrow. I need him. *(He sits down)*

(The TYPIST appears. She carries a suitcase. She crosses the stage and half way turns back rapidly)

TYPIST

>Did you call me?

YOUNG MAN

>*(Closing his eyes)* No. I didn't call you.

(The TYPIST leaves looking anxious, waiting for the call)

TYPIST

>*(By the door)* Do you need me?

YOUNG MAN

>*(Closing his eyes)* No. I don't need you.

(The TYPIST exits)

FRIEND 2

>*(In his sleep)*

I'm back for my wings,

Allow me to return.

I want to die seeing dawn break,

I want to die being yesterday.

YOUNG MAN

It's too late. Juan, switch on the lights. What's the time?

JUAN

(With intent.) Six o'clock, sir.

YOUNG MAN

All right.

FRIEND 2

(In his sleep)

I'm back for my wings,

Allow me to return

I want to die being a spring,

I want to die outside the sea...

(The YOUNG MAN taps his fingers on the table.)

SLOW CURTAIN

ACT II

(An alcove, 1900 style. Strange furniture. Grand pleated curtains full of tassels. Painted clouds and angels cover the walls. Centre, a bed with heavily decorated with plumes. Left, a dressing table sustained by angels with bouquets of electric flowers in their hands. The balconies are open, and the moon shines through them. We hear a furious car's horn. The BRIDE jumps out of the bed, wearing a splendid robe full of lace and enormous pink ribbons. She wears a long train and ringlets in her hair.)

BRIDE *(looking down the balcony)*

Come up. *(The horn is heard)* You must. My fiancee - the old man, the lyricist will arrive and I need to lean on you.

(The AMERICAN FOOTBALL PLAYER enters through the balcony. He's wearing kneepads and helmet. He carries a bag full of cigars which he constantly lights and steps on.)

BRIDE

Come in. I haven't seen you in two days.

(They embrace. The PLAYER does not talk, he only smokes and then steps on the cigar. He shows great vitality and hugs the bride impetuously)

BRIDE

You're kissing me in a different manner. It's always different, my love. You know, I didn't see you yesterday. Instead I watched the horse. Beautiful, white, with its golden hoofs amongst the stable's hay. *(They sit on a sofa at the end of the bed)* But you are more beautiful. Because you are like a dragon. *(She embraces him)* It feels like I will snap in your arms because I'm fragile, because I'm small, because I'm frost, because I'm like a small guitar burnt by the sun, and yet I don't snap. *(The PLAYER blows smoke in her face. She caresses his body)* Behind this shadow there is a net of silver bridges ready to squeeze me, tiny as a button, small as a bee that suddenly enters the throne room. True? Am I right? I'll go with you. *(Leaning her head against his shoulder)* My dragon, you're my dragon. How many hearts have you got? There is a river in your chest where I will drown. I will drown...*(She looks at him)* and then you'll run away *(she cries)* and you'll leave me dead on the shores. *(The PLAYER takes another cigar to his mouth and the BRIDE lights it for him)* Oh! *(She kisses him)* White ash, look at the ivory fire burning from your teeth. My other boyfriend had cold teeth; when he kissed me, his lips would be covered with small, dry leaves. His lips were dry. I cut off my plaits because he liked them, just as I go barefoot now, because you like it. Is that so? Am I right? *(He kisses her)* We must leave. My fiancée will be here soon.

VOICE, at the door

> Madam!

BRIDE

> Leave. *(She kisses him)*

VOICE

> Madam!

BRIDE *(Withdrawing from the PLAYER and adopting a distracted attitude)*

> Coming! *(Lowering her voice)* Good bye!

(The PLAYER comes back from the balcony and kisses her while lifting her in his arms)

VOICE

> Open up!

BRIDE *(changing her voice)*

> Some people have no patience!

(The PLAYER leaves through the balcony, whistling)

MAID *(entering)*

> Ay, Madam!

BRIDE

> What madam?

MAID

> Madam!

BRIDE

> What? *(She switches on the ceiling lights. A bluer light than that coming through the balcony)*

MAID

> Your fiancée is here!

BRIDE

> All right. So why are you getting all heated up?

MAID *(crying)*

> I don't know.

BRIDE

> Where is he?

MAID

> Downstairs.

BRIDE

> With whom?

MAID

    Your father.

BRIDE

    Is that all?

MAID

    And with a man wearing golden spectacles. They were arguing.

BRIDE

    I'll get dressed.

MAID

    Ay, Madam!

BRIDE *(angry)*

    What madam?

MAID

    Madam!

BRIDE

    What?

MAID

    Your fiancée is very handsome.

BRIDE

    You marry him then.

MAID

    He looks very happy.

BRIDE *(ironically)*

    Does he?

MAID

    He brought you this bouquet.

BRIDE

You know I don't like flowers. Throw them out of the window.

MAID

They're so beautiful! They've just been picked.

BRIDE *(with authority)*

Throw them away.

(The MAID picks the flowers from a vase and throws them out of the window/balcony)

MAID

Ay, Madam!

BRIDE *(very angry)*

What madam?

MAID

Madam!

BRIDE

Whaaaaaat?

MAID

Think about what you're doing! Think it over. The world is big, but us people are small.

BRIDE

How would you know?

MAID

I know. My father went to Brazil twice, and he was so small, he fit in a suitcase. Things are forgotten, but evil remains.

BRIDE

I told you to be quiet.

MAID

Ay Madam!

BRIDE *(energetically)*

My clothes!

MAID

What are you going to do!

BRIDE

Whatever I can!

MAID

Such a good man! Waiting for you for so long! So eagerly. Five years! *(She gives her the gowns.)*

BRIDE

Did he shake your hand?

MAID *(joyfully)*

Yes; he shook my hand.

BRIDE

And how did he shake your hand?

MAID

Very gently, he barely squeezed it.

BRIDE

You see? He didn't squeeze it.

MAID

I had a boyfriend who was a soldier who used to dig his rings into me, making me bleed. That's why I sent him away!

BRIDE *(with irony)*

Really?

MAID

    Ay, madam!

BRIDE *(irritated)*

    What gown shall I wear?

MAID

    You look beautiful in your red one.

BRIDE

    I don't want to look beautiful.

MAID

    The green one.

BRIDE *(softly)*

    No.

MAID

    The orange one?

BRIDE *(strong)*

    No.

MAID

    The blue one.

BRIDE *(stronger)*

    No.

MAID

    The one with the autumn leaves.

BRIDE *(irritated and strong)*

    I said no! I want a habit the colour of the Earth for that man, a dress of bare rock with a hemp cord round my waist. *(A car's horn is heard. The BRIDE half closes her eyes and changing her expression carries on talking)* But with a crown of jasmines round my neck and my flesh squeezed by a veil wet from the sea. *(She moves towards the balcony)*

MAID

Don't let your fiancée find out!

BRIDE

He must. *(Choosing a simple dress)* This one. *(She puts it on.)*

MAID

You're wrong!

BRIDE

Why?

MAID

Your fiancée looks for something else. There was a young man in my village who would climb up the Church's tower so he could look closely at the moon, and his bride sent him away.

BRIDE

She did well!

MAID

He said he could see his bride's face in the moon.

BRIDE *(energetically)*

And you think that's all right? *(She finishes making up)*

MAID

Yes. When I got angry at the bell boy...

BRIDE

All ready? He was so handsome!... So handsome!... So handsome!

MAID

Of course. I gave him a hankie I embroidered with the words Love, Love, Love, and he lost it.

BRIDE

Go away.

MAID

Shall I close the balcony doors?

BRIDE

No.

MAID

The wind will burn your skin.

BRIDE

I like that. I want to turn dark. Darker than a boy. And if I
fall I won't bleed, and if I grab a blueberry bush I won't
hurt myself. They can all walk blindly on the wires. I
want to have lead in my feet. Last night I dreamt that
children grew by chance... that the strength of a kiss was
enough to kill them all. A dagger, a pair of scissors last
for ever but this chest of mine lasts for only a moment.

MAID *(listening)*

Your father's coming.

BRIDE

Put all my coloured gowns away in a suitcase.

MAID *(trembling)*

Yes.

BRIDE

And have the key to the garage ready.

MAID *(scared)*

All right.

*(The FATHER enters. He's an absent minded old man. He wears
a pair of binoculars round his neck. A white wig. Pink face. He's
wearing white gloves and a black suit. He is slightly short
sighted.)*

FATHER

Are you ready?

BRIDE *(irritated)*

What should I be ready for?

FATHER

He's here!

BRIDE

So what?

FATHER

Seeing as you are engaged and it's your life, your happiness, it would be natural that you'd be happy and determined.

BRIDE

Well I'm not.

FATHER

What?

BRIDE

I'm not happy. Are you?

FATHER

But darling, what will the man say?

BRIDE

Whatever he wants!

FATHER

He came here to marry you. You have been writing to him for the five years we traveled. You didn't dance with anyone on the transatlantic boats... You never took an interest in anyone else. Why this change?

BRIDE

I don't want to see him. I must live. He talks too much.

FATHER

Why didn't you say so before?

BRIDE

I didn't exist before. Only the earth and the sea. I'd just lie sweetly sleeping on the pillows in the train.

FATHER

That man will be in his own right to insult me. Oh, my God! Everything was ready! I even bought the wedding dress. It's in there, on the mannequin.

BRIDE

Don't talk about it. I don't want to.

FATHER

And I? And I? Don't I have the right to rest? There is a moon eclipse tonight. I won't be able to see it from the terrace. As soon as I'm angry, the blood shoots to my eyes and I can't see. What shall we do with this man?

BRIDE

Whatever you want. I don't want to see him.

FATHER *(energetically and trying to appear willingly)*

You have to fulfill your engagement!

BRIDE

I won't.

FATHER

You must!

BRIDE

No.

FATHER

Yes. *(Makes a move to hit her.)*

BRIDE *(strong)*

No.

FATHER

Everyone's against me. *(He looks at the sky through the open balcony)* The eclipse's about to start. *(He goes to the balcony)* The street lamps are out. *(In agony)* It will be beautiful! I've been waiting for it for a long time. And now I won't be able to see it. Why did you lie to him?

BRIDE

I didn't lie.

FATHER

Five years. Day by day. Oh, my God!

(The MAID rushes in and runs to the balcony. Voices are heard outside.)

MAID

They're quarrelling.

FATHER

Who?

MAID

He's already inside. *(She exits quickly)*

FATHER

What's going on?

BRIDE

Where are you going? Close that door! *(In agony)*

FATHER

But why?

BRIDE

Ah!

ʃNG MAN appears. He's casually dressed. He fixes his
? enters, all the lights come up, including the bouquets
_ ..ʃ ɪne angels are holding. The three characters are left
looking at each other in silence.)

YOUNG MAN

Excuse me... *(Pause)*

FATHER *(embarrassed)*

Please sit down.

(The MAID enters nervously with her hands across her chest)

YOUNG MAN *(shaking the BRIDE's hand)*

It's been a long journey.

BRIDE *(staring at him, without letting go of his hand)*

Yes. A cold journey. It snowed a lot these past years. *(She lets go of his hand.)*

YOUNG MAN

I hope you'll forgive me, but I'm shaking from running down the street and up the stairs. And then... I beat up a couple of kids who were stoning a cat to death.

(The FATHER offers him a chair)

BRIDE *(To the MAID)*

A cold hand. A hand of wax.

MAID

He'll hear you!

BRIDE

And an old fashioned look. A look that cracks like the wing of a dry butterfly.

YOUNG MAN

No, I can't sit down. I'd rather chat. Suddenly, as I ran up the stairs, all these songs I'd forgotten came to mind, and I wanted to sing them all. *(He comes close to the BRIDE)* The plaits...

BRIDE

I never wore plaits.

YOUNG MAN

It must have been the moonlight. It must have been the air covered in lips ready to kiss your mouth.

(The MAID moves to a corner. The FATHER goes out onto the balcony and looks through his binoculars.)

BRIDE

Weren't you a bit taller?

YOUNG MAN

No.

BRIDE

Didn't you have a violent smile which sat like a claw upon your face?

YOUNG MAN

No.

BRIDE

And didn't you play rugby?

YOUNG MAN

Never.

BRIDE *(passionately)*

> And didn't you carry a horse by its mane and killed three thousand pheasants in one day?

YOUNG MAN

> Never.

BRIDE

> So! What are you here for? Your hands were full of rings. Where is that drop of blood?

YOUNG MAN

> I'll shed it if you like.

BRIDE *(energetically)*

> It's not your blood! It's mine!

YOUNG MAN

> From now on no-one will be able to pull my arms away from your neck.

BRIDE

> They're not your arms, they're mine. It is I who wants to burn away in some other fire.

YOUNG MAN

> There is no fire but my own. *(He embraces her)* Because I waited for you and now I have my dream. Your plaits are no longer a dream because I'll make them from your hair, and neither is this waist where my blood sings a dream, because this blood is now mine, slowly earned through the rain, and this dream, is mine.

BRIDE *(pulling away)*

> Leave me alone! You could've said anything but the word dream. One can't dream here! I don't want to dream... This roof will keep me safe.

YOUNG MAN

But one can love!

BRIDE

And one can not love. Go!

YOUNG MAN

What? *(Scared)*

BRIDE

Look for another woman's hair to braid.

YOUNG MAN *(as if waking up)*

No!

BRIDE

How can I let you into my alcove when someone else already did?

YOUNG MAN

Ay! *(He covers his face with his hands.)*

BRIDE

Just two days have been enough to make me feel like I'm in chains. Inside the mirrors and inside the bed sheets I can hear the whining of a boy who's following me.

YOUNG MAN

But my house's been built. With walls I built by myself. Am I supposed to allow the air live in it?

BRIDE

Am I to blame? Do you want me to go and live with you?

YOUNG MAN *(sitting on a chair, worn out)*

Yes, yes, do come.

BRIDE

A mirror, a table would be closer to you.

YOUNG MAN

What am I going to do?

BRIDE

Love.

YOUNG MAN

Who?

BRIDE

Look around. In the streets. In the country.

YOUNG MAN *(energetically)*

I won't look around. I've got you. You're here in my hands, at this very moment and you can't close the door on me because I'm wet from a five year long rain. And because later there'll be nothing, later I won't be able to love, cause everything will end later.

BRIDE

Let go!

YOUNG MAN

It's not your cheating that hurts. You're nothing. You don't mean anything. It's my lost treasure. It's my love without an end. But you'll come!

BRIDE

I won't.

YOUNG MAN

So that I won't have to start all over again. I'm even beginning to forget my words.

BRIDE

I *WON'T* go!

YOUNG MAN

So I won't die. You hear me? So I won't die.

BRIDE

Leave me alone!

MAID *(coming in)*

>Madam! *(The YOUNG MAN lets go)* Sir!

FATHER (coming in)

>Who's screaming?

BRIDE

>No -one.

FATHER *(looking at the YOUNG MAN)*

>Sir...

YOUNG MAN *(worn out)*

>We were talking.

BRIDE *(to her father)*

>I must return his presents. *(The YOUNG MAN makes a move)* All of them. It wouldn't be fair... all... except the fans... because they broke.

YOUNG MAN *(remembering)*

>Two fans.

BRIDE

>One blue...

YOUNG MAN

>With three sinking gondolas...

BRIDE

>And one white...

YOUNG MAN

>With a tiger's head in the middle. And.. are they broken?

MAID

>The miner's son took the last ribs.

FATHER

>They were good fans but...

YOUNG MAN *(smiling)*

> It doesn't matter if they got lost. They now fan the air that burns my skin.

MAID *(to the BRIDE)*

> The wedding dress too?

BRIDE

> Of course.

MAID

> It's inside, on the mannequin.

FATHER *(to the YOUNG MAN)*

> I would like to...

YOUNG MAN

> It's all right.

FATHER

> In any case, make yourself at home.

YOUNG MAN

> Thank you!

FATHER *(always looking through the balcony)*

> It must be starting.... Excuse me... *(To the BRIDE)* Coming?

BRIDE

> Yes. *(to the MAN)* Good bye!

YOUNG MAN

> Good bye! *(The others leave)*

VOICE *from outside*

> Good bye!

YOUNG MAN

> Goodbye... what now? What to do with the unknown hour to come? Where do I go?

(The light dims. The bulbs from the angels give a blue light. Moonlight enters through the balcony, which will increase through the scene. A cry is heard.)

YOUNG MAN *(looking at the door)*

Who…?

(The MANNEQUIN enters with the wedding gown. This character has a grey face and golden lips and eyebrows, like a MANNEQUIN from the window of a luxury shop. It wears a wig and golden gloves. It wears, with a certain shyness, a splendid white wedding dress, with a long tail and a veil.)

MANNEQUIN *(sings and cries)*

Who will use the shiny silver

Of the little and dark bride?

My tail is lost in the sea

And the moon wants to wear

The crown belonging to me.

My ring, sir, my ring of ancient gold

Was buried in the sands of that glass of old.

Who will wear my gown? Who will?

The big river will wear it to marry the sea.

YOUNG MAN

What are you singing? Tell me.

MANNEQUIN

I sing

Of a death I never had,

Pain of a veil not in use,
Shedding tears of silk and plume.
Underwear which remains
Frozen from the dark snow
And not allowing its lace
To contend with the wild foam.
Fabrics which cover the flesh
The lukewarm water will gain
And in the place of a murmur,
The broken smile of the rain.
Who will now use the good dress
Of the little and dark bride?

YOUNG MAN

The dark wind will wear it
At daybreak, playing in its cave,
To the reeds, velvet suspenders,
The moon, silk stockings he gave.
Give the veil now to the spiders
So that with their threads of beauty
They may wrap and they may eat
The tangled doves in their webs.
Nobody will wear your dress
With its white form and blurred light,
Where pure silk and deep frost
Gave it its shape overnight.

MANNEQUIN

My tail is lost in the sea.

YOUNG MAN

And the moon wants to wear your blossom crown in the
air.

MANNEQUIN *(Irritated)*

Don't want to! My silks are

One by one and thread by thread

Anxious for the wedding heat

And my blouse wants to know

When it will feel those warm hands

Which pressing the waist should meet.

YOUNG MAN

I'm asking too! Shut up!

MANNEQUIN

You lie. You're to blame.

You could've been for me

A horse of lead and foam,

The air breaking in your mouth

And your back leading the sea.

You could've been the loud neigh

But you are a dormant plain,

Covered in dry leaves and moss,

Where this white dress will decay.

My ring, sir, my ring of ancient gold.

YOUNG MAN

Was buried in the sands of that glass of old!

MANNEQUIN

Why didn't you come here before?

She waited for you, undressed

Like a serpent of the wind

Which is fainting at the ends.

YOUNG MAN

Silence. Leave me. Go!

Or I will furiously break

Those initials of nard

Which under the white silk hide.

Out into the streets to look

For the shoulders of a virgin bride,

Or guitars who'll sing to you

Six long, sharp music cries.

No one will wear your gown.

MANNEQUIN

I'll follow you for ever.

YOUNG MAN

Never!

MANNEQUIN

Let me speak to you!

YOUNG MAN

It's useless!

I don't want to know!

MANNEQUIN

Hear me out.

Look.

YOUNG MAN

What?

MANNEQUIN

A small dress

I stole from the dressmaker.

(She shows him a pink dress)

Two fountains of white milk

Dampen my agonising silks

And the white stinging of bees

Cover with lightning my neck.

My child. I want my child!

This sash, which from sheer joy

Out of my cold waist bursts,

Is drawing the child on my skirts.

And it's your child!

YOUNG MAN *(Taking the dress)*

Yes, my child:

Where mad dream birds arrive

To mate with sane jasmines.

(In agony)

If my child doesn't arrive,

Bird flying through the air

Can no longer sing?

MANNEQUIN

It can't.

YOUNG MAN

If my child doesn't arrive,

Boat which cruises the sea

Can no longer swim?

MANNEQUIN

It can't.

YOUNG MAN

> Stand still, harp of the rain

> As the sea turned to stone

> Laughs with its last dark wave.

MANNEQUIN

> Who will wear my gown? Who will?

YOUNG MAN *(Enthusiastically and forthright)*

> A woman who waits by the shore of the sea.

MANNEQUIN

> She's always waiting, remember?

> She was hiding in your house.

> She loved you but she left you.

> Your child sings in her warm cradle

> And being a child of the snow

> Is awaiting for your blood.

> Run, in search of her, quick!

> And bring her to me, naked,

> So that my silks will,

> One by one and thread by thread,

> Open the rose that now covers

> Her empty womb of fair flesh.

YOUNG MAN

> I must live.

MANNEQUIN

> Without waiting!

YOUNG MAN

> My child sings in her warm cradle,

And being a child of the snow

It waits for my help and warmth.

MANNEQUIN

Give me the dress!

YOUNG MAN (sweetly)

No.

MANNEQUIN *(grabbing it)*

I want it!

Whilst you search and defeat

I will sing a quiet song

Over its wrinkles sweet. *(She kisses it)*

YOUNG MAN

Hurry! Where is she?

MANNEQUIN

Out in the street.

YOUNG MAN

Before the crimson moon

Polishes its perfect curve

With blood from its own eclipse,

I'll bring naked, trembling with love,

My very own wife to be.

(The light is an intense blue. The MAID enters left, with a candelabra and the scene returns slowly to its normal light, bearing in mind the blue light from the open balcony at the far end. As the MAID appears, the MANNEQUIN freezes as in a pose at a window. Tilted head, and hands in a very delicate pose. The MAID places the candelabra on the table. Always sorrowful/remorseful and looking at the YOUNG MAN. At this moment the OLD MAN appears through a door at the right. The light grows.)

YOUNG MAN *(surprised)*

> You!

OLD MAN *(shaken, and taking his hands to his chest. He carries a silk handkerchief in his hand.)*

> Yes! Me!

(The MAID hurries to the balcony)

YOUNG MAN *(bitter)*

> I don't need you.

OLD MAN

> More than ever. Ay, you wounded me! Why did you come up? I knew what would happen. Ay!

YOUNG MAN *(sweetly, approaching the OLD MAN)*

> What's the matter?

OLD MAN *(energised)*

> Nothing. Nothing's the matter. A wound but... blood dries up and what's past is past. *(The YOUNG MAN begins to leave)* Where are you going?

YOUNG MAN *(happy)*

> Searching.

OLD MAN

> For whom?

YOUNG MAN

> For the woman who loves me. You saw her at my house, can't you remember?

OLD MAN *(harsh)*

> I can't remember anything. But wait.

YOUNG MAN

>No! Now.

(The OLD MAN grabs him by the arm)

FATHER *(Coming in)*

>Daughter! Where are you? Daughter!

(We hear the horn of a car)

MAID *(at the balcony)*

>Madam! Madam!

FATHER *(going to the balcony)*

>Daughter. Wait, wait!

(He exits)

YOUNG MAN

>I'm leaving as well! I'll look around, like her, for the new flower in my blood! *(He exits running)*

OLD MAN

>Wait! Wait! Don't leave me here, wounded! Wait! *(He exits, his cries are eventually lost)*

(The horn of a car is heard. The scene becomes blue and the MANNEQUIN approaches, hurt. With two expressions. It is impulsively asking in the first line. She answers in the second, as if far away.)

MANNEQUIN

My ring, sir! My ring of ancient gold. *(Pause)*
It was buried in the sands of that glass of old.
Who will wear my gown? Who will?
The big river will wear it to marry the sea.

(It faints and remains lying on the sofa)

VOICE *(outside)*

Waaaaait!

CURTAIN

ACT III

(A forest. Enormous trunks. Centre, a theatre surrounded by baroque curtains, its curtain down. A ladder connects the stage and the auditorium. As the curtain rises, two figures dressed in black, with white hands and faces cross the stage. A distant music is heard. The HARLEQUIN appears, dressed in black and green. He carries two masks: one in each hand, behind his back. He gestures in a rhythmic way, like a dancer.)

HARLEQUIN

    The Dream rides on Time

    Like a boat in the sea.

    No one can sow all the seeds

    Within the heart of the Dream.

(He wears a mask with a very happy expression)

    Look how the daybreak sings! See how it sings!

    As icicles of blue frost it lifts.

(He removes the mask)

    Time rides on the Dream

    Covered up to its head.

    Yesterday and today

    Dark mourning flowers they ate.

(He wears a mask with a sleepy face)

Look how the night sings! See how it sings!

As a grove of anemones it lifts!

(He removes it)

Around the same pillar

Lie entwined the Dream and Time,

Just like the tongue of a man,

Cuts through the cry of a child.

(With a mask)

Look how the daybreak sings! See how it sings!

(With the other)

As a grove of anemones lifts!

And if the Dream raises walls

Against the grassland of Time,

Time will make him believe

He will be born in a while.

Look how the night sings! See how it sings!

As icicles of blue frost it lifts.

(From this moment, during the whole act and at calculated times, distant deep horns will be heard. A GIRL appears, dressed in black. She's skipping with a rope)

GIRL

> Who can tell,
>
> Who will tell me?
>
> My lover awaits
>
> Under the sea.

HARLEQUIN

> *(Making fun)* Not true.

GIRL

> True.
>
> My wish I have lost
>
> My thimble before -
>
> amongst the big trunks
>
> I found them once more.

HARLEQUIN

> *(Ironically)* A very long rope.

GIRL

> Long, to go below.
>
> Sharks and fish,
>
> And coral branches.

HARLEQUIN

> He's below.

GIRL

> Deep down below.

HARLEQUIN

> Asleep.

GIRL

> He's below!

By flags of water green

As Captain he'll be seen.

HARLEQUIN

(Loudly and jokingly) Not true.

GIRL

True.

I lost my thimble,

I lost my crown,

As I turned the corner

Both of them I found.

HARLEQUIN

Just now.

GIRL

Now?

HARLEQUIN

Your lover you'll see

As you turn the corner

Round the wind and the sea.

GIRL

(Scared) Not true.

HARLEQUIN

True.

I'll give him to you.

GIRL

(Uneasy) You won't give him to me.

No one ever reaches

The bed of the sea.

HARLEQUIN

    (Loudly, as if he were in the circus) Mister man, come here!

(A CLOWN appears. His powdered face reminds one of a skull. He laughs loudly)

HARLEQUIN

    You'll give this young girl....

CLOWN

    Her boyfriend from the sea.

    (Rolling his sleeves) Give me a ladder.

GIRL

    (Scared) Why?

CLOWN

    (To the GIRL) To go down.

    (To audience) Good evening!

HARLEQUIN

    Bravo!

CLOWN

    (To HARLEQUIN) You look that way! *(The HARLEQUIN turns, laughing)* Come on, play! *(He claps)*

HARLEQUIN

    I play! *(He plays a white violin with golden strings. It must be big and flat. He sings)*

CLOWN *(Keeping the beat with his head)*

    Boyfriend, where are you?

HARLEQUIN *(Changing his voice)*

    Through the fresh seaweed

    I'm going to hunt

Enormous sea snails

And iris of salt.

GIRL *(Screaming, scared of the reality of it all)*

I don't want to!

CLOWN

Silence! *(HARLEQUIN laughs)*

GIRL *(Scared, to the CLOWN)*

Over tall bushes

Jumping I'll be.

And then we will swim

Within the blue green.

HARLEQUIN *(Jocose and turning)*

Not true!

GIRL

True!

(She starts to leave, crying)

Who can tell,

Who will tell me?

My thimble and crown

I lost in the sea.

HARLEQUIN *(Melancholic)*

Around the corner

From the wind and the sea.

(The GIRL exits)

CLOWN *(Pointing)*

There.

HARLEQUIN

     Where? What?

CLOWN

     To perform.

     A little boy

     Who wants to change

     Into steel flowers

     His small bit of bread.

HARLEQUIN

     (Slightly incredulous) Not true.

CLOWN

     (Severely) True.

     I lost rose and crown,

     My necklace, before;

     And amongst the ivory

     I found them once more.

HARLEQUIN

     Mister Man! Come along! *(He starts to leave)*

CLOWN

(Shouting and looking at the forest, and ahead of the HARLEQUIN)

     Not so much shouting.

     Good morning! *(Quietly)* Let's go!

     (Aloud) Play!

HARLEQUIN

     Play?

CLOWN

A waltz. *(HARLEQUIN starts playing. Softly.)* Hurry up. *(Aloud)* Ladies and gentlemen, I will now show..

HARLEQUIN

That amongst the ivory

I found them as so.

CLOWN

You will now see... *(Exits)*

HARLEQUIN *(Exiting)*

The wheel that spins

'Tween the wind and the sea.

(Horns are heard. The TYPIST enters. She wears a tennis outfit, with a bright coloured beret. On top of her costume she wears a cape of a single gauze. The MASK is with her. She wears a 1900 gown, of a bright yellow with a long tail, hair of yellow silk, which falls like a shawl, her mask is of white plaster, with elbow high gloves of the same colour. She wears a yellow hat and her chest is covered in golden sequins. The effect of this character must be that of a sudden flame over the lunar blues and nightl;y trunks. She speaks with a slight Italian accent.)

MASK

(Laughing) A true darling.

TYPIST

I left his house. I remember on the afternoon of my departure there was a heavy summer downpour and the housekeeper's son had died. I went through the library and he said "Did you call?"; to which I answered, closing my eyes "NO!". Then, near the door, he said, "Do you need me?" and I said "No. I don't need you."

MASK

Beautiful!

TYPIST

He'd wait up all night until I showed myself at the window.

MASK

And you, signorina typist...?

TYPIST

I never did. But... I could see him through the cracks... still! *(She takes out a handkerchief)* With such eyes! The air came in like a knife, but I couldn't talk to him.

MASK

"Puor que señorina?"

TYPIST

Because he loved me too much.

MASK

Oh "mio Dio"! Just like Count Arturo from Italy. Oh, my love!

TYPIST

Really?

MASK

In the foyer of the Paris Opera there are some enormous banisters overlooking the sea. Count Arturo, a camellia between his lips, would arrive in a small boat with his son, both abandoned by me. But I would draw back the curtains and throw a diamond at them. Oh, "que dolchisimo tormento, amica mia". *(Weeping)* The count and his boy went without eating and would sleep amongst the branches of a tree, which a Russian had given me. *(Energetic and pleading)* Don't you have a piece of bread for me? Don't you have a piece of bread for my son? For the boy Count Arturo let die in the frost? *(Shaken)* And then I went to the hospital, where I learnt, the Count had married a great Roman lady... and from then on I have begged and shared my bed with the men who unload coal in the bay.

TYPIST

What are you saying? Why do you speak like that?

MASK

(Calming down) What I'm trying to say is that Count Arturo loved me so much he'd cry with his son behind the curtains, while I was like a silver half moon, amongst the binoculars and gaslights which glowed under the dome of the Paris Opera.

TYPIST

Delicious. When is the Count arriving?

MASK

When does your "amico" arrive?

TYPIST

He'll take time. Never means immediately.

MASK

Arturo will also be late immediately. On his right hand he has a scar they made with a dagger... because of me, of course. *(Showing her hand)* Can't you see? *(Pointing at her neck)* There's another one here, you see?

TYPIST

Yes! But why?

MASK

"¿Per qué? ¿Per qué?" What would I do without wounds? Who do the Count's wounds belong to?

TYPIST

To you. It's true! He's been waiting for me for five years, but... how beautiful it is to wait in certainty for the moment in which one will be loved!

MASK

>And it's true?

TYPIST

>It's true! That's why we can laugh! As a child, I'd keep the sweets so I could eat them later.

MASK

>Ha, ha, ha! Really? They taste better!

TYPIST

>*(Starting to exit)* If my friend comes - tall, with curly hair, but curled in a special way - pretend not to know him.

MASK

>Of course, "amica mia"!

(The YOUNG MAN enters)

HARLEQUIN

>Hey!

YOUNG MAN

>What?

HARLEQUIN

>Where are you going?

YOUNG MAN

>Home.

HARLEQUIN

>*(Ironically)* Is that so?

YOUNG MAN

>Of course! *(Starts walking)*

HARLEQUIN

Hey! You can't go that way!

YOUNG MAN

Did they ring the park?

HARLEQUIN

The circus is there.

YOUNG MAN

All right. *(He turns)*

HARLEQUIN

Full of perfectly still spectators. *(Smoothly)* Won't Sir go in?

YOUNG MAN

(Shaken) No. *(Not wanting to listen)* Has the elm street also been cut off?

HARLEQUIN

That's where the carts and the serpent cages are.

YOUNG MAN

Then I'll go back. *(Starts to exit)*

CLOWN *(entering)*

But where is he going? Ha, ha, ha!

HARLEQUIN

He says he's going home.

CLOWN

(Giving the HARLEQUIN a circus slap) Have a home!

HARLEQUIN

(Falls to the ground screaming) Ay, it hurts, it hurts! Ayyy!

CLOWN

(To the YOUNG MAN) Come on!

YOUNG MAN

(Irritated) Can you tell me what kind of a joke this is? I was going home, I mean not my home; another home, to...

CLOWN

(Interrupting) To look around.

YOUNG MAN

Yes. Because I need to. Look around.

CLOWN

(Happy) Look around? Turn around, and it will be found!

TYPIST'S VOICE *(singing)*

Where are you going, my love?

My love!

With the air in a glass

and the sea in a cup?

(The HARLEQUIN has got up. The CLOWN signals to him. The YOUNG MAN has his back turned, and they leave without turning their back, on tiptoe, dancing and with their fingers on their lips. The lights in the theatre come up.)

YOUNG MAN *(surprised)*

Where are you going, my love?

My life, my love,

With the air in a glass

and the sea in a cup?

TYPIST

Where? Where I'm called!

YOUNG MAN

My life!

TYPIST

    With you.

YOUNG MAN

    I must take you, naked,

    Withered flower, body clean

    To the place where the silk

    Shivers in the cold.

    White sheets will await you.

    Let's go soon. Let's leave now.

    Before yellow nightingales

    Spring from the branch as a moan.

TYPIST

    Yes, because the sun is a kite.

    Better still: a hawk of glass.

    No: the sun is a big trunk

    And you the shadow of a brook.

    And how come lilies and reeds

    Do not grow where I am held,

    And the colour of my dress

    Your precious waves cannot fade?

    Love, abandon me on the mountain,

    Covered in clouds and dew

    So I can watch you, sad and looming,

    Covering a dormant sky.

YOUNG MAN

    Don't talk like that! Girl! Let's go.

    I don't want time to be lost:

    Pure blood and deep heat

Drive me to some other place.

I want to live.

TYPIST

With whom?

YOUNG MAN

With you.

TYPIST

What's that I hear from so afar?

YOUNG MAN

The day returning, my love.

My love!

TYPIST *(joyfully, as in a dream)*

A nightingale- let it sing!

A grey bird in the afternoon

On the branch of a maple tree.

I felt you, nightingale.

I want to live.

YOUNG MAN

Who with?

TYPIST

With the shadow of a brook.

(In agony, seeking refuge in the YOUNG MAN's chest)

What's that I hear from so afar?

YOUNG MAN

Love.

The blood in my throat.

My love.

TYPIST

> For ever this way, for ever,
>
> Awake or asleep.

YOUNG MAN *(energetic, with passion)*

> Never this way, never, never.
>
> Let's leave this place.

TYPIST

> Wait!

YOUNG MAN

> Love doesn't wait!

TYPIST

> Where are you going my love?
>
> With love in a glass
>
> And the sea in a cup.

(The TYPIST goes to the staircase. The library from the first act appears, reduced and in pale colours. The MASK appears. She has an embroidered hankie in her hand, and she breathes in constantly from a flask of salts, as she weeps.)

MASK *(To the TYPIST)*

> I have just abandoned the Count for ever. He was left behind with his son. *(Coming down the stairs)* I'm sure he'll die. But he loves me so much! So much! *(She cries. To the TYPIST)* Don't you know? His boy will die under the frost. I left him! Can't you see how happy I am! Can't you see how I'm laughing? *(She cries)* Now he'll look everywhere for me. *(On the floor)* I'll hide amongst the blueberry bushes, *(loudly)* inside the blueberry bushes. I speak like this because I don't want Arturo to know where I am. *(Loudly)* I don't love you! I told you I don't love

you! *(She exits, crying)* You love me, but I, don't love you.

(Two SERVANTS appear, in blue uniforms and very pale faces. They place two white stools stage left. JUAN crosses the small stage, always on tiptoe.)

TYPIST

> *(To JUAN, climbing up to the small stage)* If my former master comes, let him in. *(On the stage)* Although he won't come, until he must.

(The YOUNG MAN starts climbing up the ladder)

YOUNG MAN

> *(On the stage, passionately)* Are you happy here?

TYPIST

> Did you write those letters?

YOUNG MAN

> One is better upstairs. Come over!

TYPIST

> I've loved you so much!

YOUNG MAN

> I love you so much!

TYPIST

> I'll love you so much!

YOUNG MAN

> I'm in agony without you. Where will I go if you leave me? I can't remember anything. The other one, she doesn't exist, but you do, because you love me.

ed you, love! I'll always love you.

TYPIST

Why do you say now?

(The OLD MAN appears on the big stage. He's dressed in blue and has a big handkerchief in his hand, stained with blood, which he takes to his face and chest. He is agitated and watches attentively what is going on)

YOUNG MAN

I waited. I was dying.

TYPIST

I was dying of waiting.

YOUNG MAN

But my blood beats in my temples with its knuckles of fire, and now I've got you here.

VOICE *offstage*

My son! My son!

(The DEAD BOY crosses the small stage, on his own)

YOUNG MAN

Yes, my son! He runs inside me, like a lonely ant inside a closed box. *(To the TYPIST)* A bit of light for my boy! Please! He is so small! He presses his nose against the glass of my heart, and yet, he can't breathe.

MASK *(appearing on the BIG STAGE)*

> My son!

(Two more MASKS appear, watching the scene)

TYPIST *(Dry, with authority)*

> Did you write those letters? It's not your son, it's me. You
> waited and let me go, but you always thought you were
> loved. Am I lying?

YOUNG MAN *(Impatiently)*

> No, but...

TYPIST

> I, however, knew you'd never love me. And yet, I lifted
> my love and changed you and I saw you round every
> corner of my house. I love you, but far away from you.
> I've been running away for so long, that I need to watch
> the sea to evoke the trembling of your lips.

OLD MAN

> Because if he is twenty years old, he can be twenty
> moons.

TYPIST

> *(Lyrically)* Twenty rocks, twenty northern snowfalls.

YOUNG MAN

> *(Irritated)* Shut up. You'll come with me. Because you
> love me and because it's necessary that I stay alive.

TYPIST

> Yes, I love you, but much more. You don't have the eyes
> to see me naked, nor the mouth to kiss my endless body.
> Leave me alone. I love you too much to admire you.

YOUNG MAN

Not one minute more! Come on! *(He seizes her by the wrists)*

TYPIST

You're hurting me, love.

YOUNG MAN

And so you'll feel me.

TYPIST

(Sweetly) Wait... I'll go... For ever. *(He embraces him)*

OLD MAN

She'll go. Sit down, my friend. Wait.

YOUNG MAN

(In agony) NO.

TYPIST

(Holding him) I climbed too high. Why did you leave me? I was going to die of cold and I had to look for your love where there weren't any people. But I'll be with you. Let me come down slowly towards you.

(The CLOWN and HARLEQUIN appear, carrying a concertina and a white violin respectively. They sit down on the white stools.)

CLOWN

Music.

HARLEQUIN

Of years.

CLOWN

Moons and rivers unopened.

Left behind?

HARLEQUIN

The wind's veil.

CLOWN

And the music from your violin.

YOUNG MAN

(Coming out of a dream) Come on!

TYPIST

Yes... is it really you? So suddenly...! Without having slowly savoured this lovely idea: tomorrow will be. Don't you feel pity for me?

YOUNG MAN

Upstairs there's something like a nest. One can hear a nightingale sing... and even if it can't be heard, even if the bat beats its wings against the glass!

TYPIST

Yes. Yes, but...

YOUNG MAN

(Energetically) Your mouth! *(He kisses her)*

TYPIST

Later...

YOUNG MAN

(Passionately) It's better at night.

TYPIST

I'll leave!

YOUNG MAN

Without delay!

TYPIST

I want to! Listen.

YOUNG MAN

Let's go!

TYPIST

But...

YOUNG MAN

Tell me.

TYPIST

I'll come with you...!

YOUNG MAN

Love!

TYPIST

I'll come with you. *(Shy)* When five years pass!

YOUNG MAN

Ay! *(He takes his hands to his forehead)*

OLD MAN

(Softly) Bravo.

(The YOUNG MAN begins slowly to come down the ladder. The TYPIST remains static on the stage. JUAN comes out on tiptoe and covers her with a large white cape)

CLOWN

Music.

HARLEQUIN

Of years.

CLOWN

Moons and rivers unopened.

A music left behind.

HARLEQUIN

The wind's veil.

CLOWN

And the music from your violin.

(They play)

MASK

The Count kisses my Amazon portrait.

OLD MAN

We are going to not get there, but we're going to go.

YOUNG MAN

(Desperate, to the CLOWN) The exit, where?

TYPIST

(On the small stage, as if in a dream) My love! My love!

YOUNG MAN

(Trembling) Show me the door!

CLOWN

(Ironically, pointing to the left) That way.

HARLEQUIN

(Pointing to the right) That way.

TYPIST

I'll wait, love! I'll wait! Come back soon!

HARLEQUIN

(Ironically) That way!

YOUNG MAN *(To the CLOWN)*

I'll break your cages and your tents.

I know how to jump the wall.

OLD MAN

(In agony) This way.

YOUNG MAN

I want to go back! Leave me alone.

HARLEQUIN

The wind remains!

CLOWN

And the music from your violin!

CURTAIN

ACT III - last scene

(The same library as in the first act. Left, the wedding gown on the mannequin without head or arms. Several open suitcases. Enter the MAID and JUAN)

MAID

> *(Amazed)* Really?

JUAN

> She's now a housekeeper, but she used to be a great lady. She lived with a very rich Italian Count for a very long time, father of the child they just buried.

MAID

> Poor thing! He looked so lovely.

JUAN

> It was then she acquired the habits of the rich. That's why she spent everything she had on the boy's clothes and the box.

MAID

> And the flowers! I gave her a small bunch of roses, but they were so small they didn't even take them into the room.

YOUNG MAN

> *(Coming in)* Juan.

JUAN

> Sir.

(The MAID exits)

YOUNG MAN

Bring me a cool glass of water. *(The YOUNG MAN shows great desperation and physical weakness. JUAN serves him)* Wasn't that window much larger?

JUAN

No.

YOUNG MAN

It's amazing it's so narrow. My house used to have an enormous patio where I'd play with my little rocking horse. The last time I saw it, I was twenty, and it seemed so small it was incredible that I once flew around it.

JUAN

Is Sir feeling well?

YOUNG MAN

Does a fountain giving water feel well? Answer.

JUAN

(Smiling) I don't know...

YOUNG MAN

Does a weather vane spinning as the wind wants feel well?

JUAN

Sir gives such examples... but I would ask, if Sir allows... does the wind feel well?

YOUNG MAN

(Dry) I feel well.

JUAN

Did you rest after your trip?

YOUNG MAN

Yes.

JUAN

I celebrate it infinitely. *(He starts to exit)*

YOUNG MAN

Juan, are my clothes ready?

JUAN

Yes, sir. In your bedroom.

YOUNG MAN

What suit?

JUAN

The tails. I laid them on the bed.

YOUNG MAN

(Irritated) Then remove them. I don't want to go upstairs and find them on the bed, so big! So empty! Whoever thought of buying it. I used to have a small one, remember?

JUAN

Yes, sir. Of carved walnut.

YOUNG MAN

(Gaily) That's it! Of carved walnut. One slept so well in it! I remember, as a child, I saw a massive moon being born behind the rail at its feet... or was it through the railings in the balcony? I don't know. Where is it?

JUAN

Sir gave it away.

YOUNG MAN

(Thinking) Who to?

JUAN

(Serious) To your old typist.

(The YOUNG MAN remains pensive. Pause)

YOUNG MAN *(Indicating JUAN leave)*

> That's fine.

(JUAN exits)

YOUNG MAN *(In agony)*

> Juan!

JUAN

> *(Returning, severe.)* Sir.

YOUNG MAN

> You probably set my leather shoes...

JUAN

> The ones with the black silk bands.

YOUNG MAN

> Black silk.. No... Look for another pair. *(Rising)* Is it possible the air is always scarce in this house? I'm going to cut all the flowers in the garden, especially those dammed oleanders that jump over the walls and that grass which grows by itself at midnight.

JUAN

> They say poppies and anemones give headaches at certain times of day.

YOUNG MAN

> That's probably it. Take that as well. *(Pointing to the wedding dress)* Leave it in the attic.

JUAN

> Very well. *(About to exit)*

YOUNG MAN

> *(Shy)* And leave the leather shoes. But change the bands.

(A doorbell is heard)

JUAN

(Coming in) It's the gentlemen, they've come to play.

YOUNG MAN

(Annoyed) Open up.

JUAN *(At the door)*

Sir probably needs to get dressed.

YOUNG MAN

Yes. *(He exits almost like a shadow)*

(The PLAYERS enter. There are three of them. They are dressed in tails. They wear white capes that reach the floor.)

PLAYER 1

It happened in Venice. A bad year for gambling. But that young man could really play. He was pale, so pale that in the last round he had nothing to do but play the ace of hearts. A heart full of his blood. He played it, and when he went to pick it up *(lowering his voice)* to... *(looking at both sides)* he had an ace of diamonds, sparkling like the sun and he ran away, staring at his reflection, with two girls, down the Grand Canal.

PLAYER 2

One shouldn't trust pale people, or the weary; they play, but they keep to themselves.

PLAYER 3

I once played with an old man in India who, when he no longer had one drop of blood over his cards, and when I was about to pounce on him, he dyed all the clubs red and was able to escape amongst the foliage.

PLAYER 1

> We play and we win, but it's hard work. Cards drink rich blood from our hands and it's hard to cut the thread that binds them.

PLAYER 2

> But I think with this one... we're not mistaken.

PLAYER 3

> I'm not sure.

PLAYER 1

> *(To PLAYER 2)* You'll never learn to know your clients. This one? His life trickles down his pupils like two jets wetting the corner of his mouth, dying the front of his shirt coral red.

PLAYER 2

> Yes, but remember the boy in Sweden who played with us, almost agonising, and how we were almost blinded by the jet of blood he spurted.

PLAYER 3

> The pack of cards! *(He takes one out)*

PLAYER 2

> We must play smoothly, so he won't react.

PLAYER 1

> And even though neither the other one, nor the lady typist will ever think of coming here till five years pass, if they come at all...

PLAYER 3

> *(Laughing)* If they come!

PLAYER 1

> It wouldn't be a bad idea to be quick.

PLAYER 2

> He keeps an ace up his sleeve.

PLAYER 3

A young heart, down which arrows will probably slip.

PLAYER 1

(Happy and profound) I bought some arrows at a shooting gallery...

PLAYER 3

(Curious) Where?

PLAYER 1

(Joking) At a shooting gallery, that not only pierce through the hardest steel, but also through the finest lint. And that is hard! *(They laugh)*

PLAYER 2

(Laughing) Anyway, we'll see.

(The YOUNG MAN appears, in tails)

YOUNG MAN

Gentlemen! *(Shakes their hands)* You're very early. It's too hot.

PLAYER 1

Not that hot!

PLAYER 3 *(To the YOUNG MAN)*

Elegant as ever!

PLAYER 1

So elegant, he should never again take his clothes off.

PLAYER 2

(Interrupting) Which we can't tear from his body.

YOUNG MAN

(Annoyed) Too kind.

(JUAN appears with a tray and wine glasses he leaves on the table)

YOUNG MAN

Shall we start? *(The three sit down)*

PLAYER 1

Ready.

PLAYER 2

(Softly) You have a good eye.

PLAYER 3

Won't you sit down?

YOUNG MAN

No... I'd rather play standing up.

PLAYER 1

Standing up?

PLAYER 2

(Softly) You'll have to hurry up.

PLAYER 1

(Dealing the cards) How many?

YOUNG MAN

Four. *(Cards are dealt.)*

PLAYER 3

(Softly) Null game.

YOUNG MAN

These cards are so cold! Nothing. *(He places them on the table)* What about you?

PLAYER 1

(In a deep voice) Nothing.

PLAYER 2

    Nothing.

PLAYER 3

    Nothing.

(PLAYER 1 deals again)

PLAYER 2

    (Looking at his cards) Wonderful.

PLAYER 3

    (Looking at his cards, anxiously) Let's see!

PLAYER 1

    (To the YOUNG MAN) Your go.

YOUNG MAN

    (Happy) My go! *(He places a card on the table.)*

PLAYER 1

    (Energetically) And mine!

PLAYER 2

    And mine!

PLAYER 3

    And mine!

YOUNG MAN

    (Excited, with one card) And now....?

(The three PLAYERS show their three cards. The YOUNG MAN halts and hides the card in his hand.)

YOUNG MAN

    Juan, serve these gentlemen a drink.

PLAYER 1

(Smoothly) Will you kindly show us your card?

YOUNG MAN

(Anxious) What liquor would you like?

PLAYER 2

(Sweetly) The card...?

YOUNG MAN (To PLAYER 3)

You probably like anisette. It's a drink...

PLAYER 3

Please... the card...

YOUNG MAN (To JUAN; who is entering)

What, no whisky?

(As JUAN enters, the PLAYERS become silent, with their cards in their hands)

YOUNG MAN

Or cognac...?

PLAYER 1 (In a soft voice and hiding from JUAN)

The card.

YOUNG MAN

(Anxious) Cognac is a drink for men who know how to endure.

PLAYER 2 (Energetically, but in a soft voice)

Your card!

YOUNG MAN

Or would you prefer chartreuse?

(JUAN exits)

PLAYER 1 *(Standing up, energetically)*

    Be so kind as to play.

YOUNG MAN

    Immediately. But we must drink.

PLAYER 3 *(Strongly)*

    We must play.

YOUNG MAN

    (Anxious) Yes, yes. A bit of chartreuse. Chartreuse is like a great green moonlit night within a castle where there is a young man with golden breeches.

PLAYER 1 *(Strongly)*

    You must give us your ace.

YOUNG MAN *(Aside)*

    My heart!

PLAYER 2 *(Energetically)*

    Because one's got to win or lose. Come on. Your card!

PLAYER 3

    Come on!

PLAYER 1

    Place your bets!

YOUNG MAN *(In pain)*

    My card!

PLAYER 1

    Your last!

YOUNG MAN

    I play!

(He places the card on the table. At that moment, a big ace of hearts appears on the shelves of the library. PLAYER 1 takes out

a gun and shoots an arrow, with no sound. The ace disappears and the YOUNG MAN takes his hands to his heart.)

PLAYER 1

One must live!

PLAYER 2

One must not wait.

PLAYER 3

Cut! Cut well.

(PLAYER 1, with a pair of scissors, cuts the air a couple of times.)

PLAYER 1 *(Softly)*

Let's go.

PLAYER 2

Hurry!

PLAYER 3

One must never wait. One must live.

(They exit.)

YOUNG MAN

Juan! Juan!

ECHO

Juan! Juan!

YOUNG MAN *(Agonising)*

I lost everything.

ECHO

    I lost everything...

YOUNG MAN

    My love...

ECHO

    Love...

(The YOUNG MAN dies. JUAN appears with a lit candelabra. The clock strikes twelve)

CURTAIN

Federico García Lorca

19 August 1931

This version of 'When Five Years Pass' was first performed by
Forbidden Theatre Company in 1997 at the Chelsea Arts Centre in
London. For more information on Forbidden TC, visit
www.forbidden.org.uk

If you would like to find out more about the translator Pilar Orti,
visit www.pilarortigarces.co.uk

Made in United States
North Haven, CT
30 December 2021

13877497R00071